FOZZIE'S
BOOK OF
FUN-EE

THIS **MOST** SENSATIONAL,
INSPIRATIONAL, CELEBRATIONAL,
MUPPETATIONAL
MUPPETS JOKE BOOK
EVER!

BY
The Muppets

WITH
Brandon T. Snider

Bath · New York · Cologne · Melbourne · Delhi
Hong Kong · Shenzhen · Singapore · Amsterdam

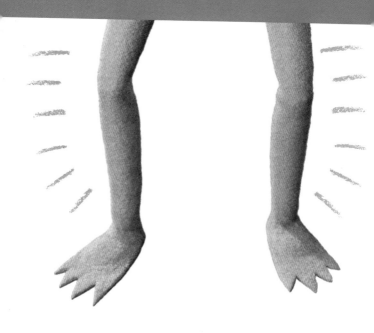

AS A TADPOLE,
I ALWAYS WANTED TO BE A DANCER

— BUT YOU KNOW WHAT THEY SAY

THE FIRST THINGS TO GO
ON A FROG

ARE HIS LEGS! ☺

I like the movie so far.

IT HASN'T
STARTED YET.

That's why
I like it! ☺

3

FOZZIE,
WHAT ARE YOU CARRYING
THE FISH FOR?

I FINALLY FOUND A
SURE WAY TO LOSE WEIGHT:

I bought a scale that lies! ☺

I HAVE A DRESSING ROOM SO SMALL...

ALL THE MICE ARE HUNCHBACKS! ☺

I'VE GOT A **JOB** FOR YOU!

OH, GOOD.

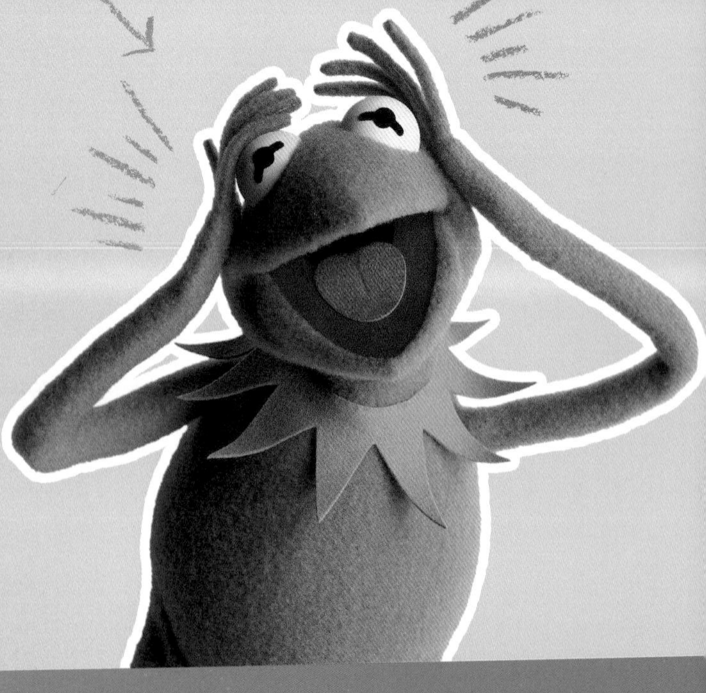

THAT GONZO IS **SO DUMB.**
HE JUST HEARD
WE'RE RUNNING SHORT ON WATER...

SO HE WANTS US TO DILUTE IT! ☺

I WOULD VERY MUCH LIKE **TO DEMONSTRATE** MY MAGNETIC **BOMB-ATTRACTOR VEST.**

WHY

DID YOU EVEN INVENT ONE OF THOSE?

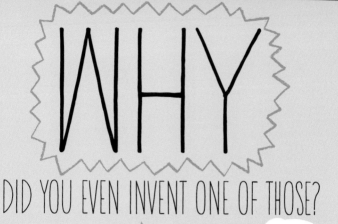

WHY DID I INVENT THE THE AUTOMATIC DROWNING HELMET? **THE EXTRA SHARP CHAIR?** THE UNEXPECTEDLY EXPLODING MUFFIN? **BECAUSE IT'S THERE, KERMIT... BECAUSE IT'S THERE.** ☺

I JUST WANT TO KNOW MORE ABOUT THIS WEDDING SKETCH I MEAN, I'VE GOT TO **learn my lines, Piggy.**

WELL, YOU ONLY HAVE ONE LINE.

I do?

EXACTLY! ☺

Hey, Kermit, KERMIT!
THIS BUNCH OF COWS
LOVES ME.
I'M A HIT!

NOT BUNCH, HERD.

Heard of what?

HERD OF COWS.

(CONT.)

COULD I HELP YOU OUT?

Please.

WHICH WAY DID YOU COME IN? ☺

21

A GUY WALKS INTO A DINER.

THERE'S A HORSE BEHIND
THE COUNTER. THE HORSE JUST
LOOKS AT THE GUY AND SAYS,

**"What's the matter?
Surprised to see me here?"**

AND THE GUY SAYS,

**" Yeah, did the cow
sell the place?"** ☺

OH, NO, ANOTHER CHICKEN!

IF THEY KEEP BRINGING IN CHICKENS WE'RE GOING TO BE HERE TWENTY-FOUR HOURS.

WHAT DO YOU MEAN?

WE'LL HAVE TO WORK AROUND THE

CLUCK! ☺

MY DEAR GONZO, I KNOW IT WILL BE PAINFUL FOR A WHILE, BUT IN TIME YOU SHALL FORGET ALL ABOUT ME.

But I already have.

OH.

YES, I FOUND SOMEBODY ELSE.

OH, UH, WELL ... UH, YEAH, WHAT, UH—
WHAT'S SHE LIKE?

WELL, SHE'S NOTHING LIKE <u>YOU</u> AT ALL.
SHE'S BEEYOOO-TIFUL!

(CONT.)

SHE'S GOT THIS CUTE LITTLE NOSE, AND SHE'S INTELLIGENT, AND TALENTED, AND I'M VERY HAPPY.

You see, breaking up with you isn't painful at all.

NOT UNTIL NOW.

HI-YAH! ☺

MY COUSIN IS
SO DUMB
HE THINKS
EGGS BENEDICT IS A

MAFIA GANGSTER!

WELCOME AGAIN TO
Muppet Labs,
where the future is being made today.
AND HERE IT IS, FOLKS,
THE PRODUCT YOU'VE
ALL BEEN WAITING FOR:

THE NEW SOLID STATE

GORILLA
DETECTOR.

Yes, friends,

HOW MANY TIMES
HAVE YOU AWAKENED AT NIGHT IN THE DARK
AND SAID TO YOURSELF,

"Is there a gorilla in here?"

AND HOW MANY PEOPLE DO
YOU KNOW WHOSE HOLIDAYS
WERE RUINED BECAUSE

THEY WERE EATEN BY
UNDETECTED
GORILLAS? ☺

YOU'RE SUCH A SMOOTH DANCER.
EVER SINCE WE'VE STARTED, I FEEL LIKE
MY FEET HAVE NEVER TOUCHED THE FLOOR.

They haven't.
You've been standing on mine. ☺

WHAT HAS A THOUSAND LEGS BUT CAN'T WALK?

Five hundred pairs of trousers! ☺

I GO OUT WITH A LOVELY GIRL.

She's so bow-legged,

WHEN SHE STANDS
AROUND THE HOUSE,

SHE STANDS

AROUND THE HOUSE! ☺

I STAYED
AT A HOTEL

so exclusive

THAT ROOM SERVICE WAS

AN UNLISTED NUMBER! ☺

IF YOU DON'T MIND,
I'LL DO THE JOKES.

We don't mind, but

WHEN ARE YOU GOING TO DO THEM? ☺

KERMIT,
ARE YOU BUSY?

YES, GONZO,
BUT I CAN GIVE YOU
MY EAR FOR A MOMENT.

WHAT WOULD I DO WITH YOUR EAR?

VAN GOGH IMPRESSIONS!

MY HOUSE IS SO DIRTY...

MY DOG BURIES HIS BONES IN THE LIVING ROOM CARPET.

ANIMAL, WILL YOU STOP BUGGING ME?

GO DO SOMETHING TO CALM DOWN. GO FIND A HOBBY OR SOMETHING!

(CONT.)

HOBBY! HOBBY!

HOBBY!

HOBBY!

HOBBY!

HOBBY!

HOBBY!

HOBBY!

HOBBY!

HOBBY!

AHEM. I WOULD JUST LIKE TO SAY A FEW WORDS ABOUT **NUDITY** IN THE WORLD TODAY. I, FOR ONE, AM JUST APPALLED BY IT.

WHY, DID YOU KNOW THAT UNDERNEATH THEIR CLOTHING, THE ENTIRE POPULATION OF THE WORLD IS WALKING AROUND COMPLETELY **NAKED?** HMM?

ISN'T THAT DISGUSTING?

AND IT'S NOT JUST PEOPLE, ALTHOUGH, GOODNESS KNOWS, THAT'S BAD ENOUGH. EVEN CUTE LITTLE DOGGIES AND PUSSYCATS CAN'T BE TRUSTED. UNDERNEATH THEIR FUR, AB-SO-LUTE-LY **NAKED!** AND IT'S NOT JUST THE QUADRUPEDS, EITHER. BIRDS, TOO! YES! BENEATH THOSE FINE FEATHERS, BIRDS WEAR

NOTHING! NOTHING AT ALL!

ABSO-... ☺

THESE TWO CANNIBALS WERE TALKING.
ONE CANNIBAL SAYS TO THE OTHER CANNIBAL,

"WHO WAS THAT LADY
I SAW YOU WITH
LAST NIGHT?"

THE OTHER CANNIBAL SAYS,

"THAT WAS NO LADY-
THAT WAS MY LUNCH!" ☺

WHATEVER HAPPENS NEXT, I WOULDN'T GIVE UP THIS EVENING FOR ANYTHING. WOULD YOU?

Make me an offer. ☺

WOULD YOU LEND
ME A **FIVER** TILL PAY DAY?
I GOTTA PAY MY WRITER,
THE LEGENDARY
'GAGS' BEASLEY.

Comes pretty cheap, doesn't he?

WELL, WE WORKED
OUT A GREAT DEAL.

(CONT.)

You pay him by the line?

NO,
I PAY HIM BY THE LAUGH.

Oh, then he owes
YOU
money! ☺

I SUGGEST WE JUMP.

Are you crazy? THAT'S AT LEAST A HUNDRED FEET!

I DIDN'T SAY
IT WAS A GOOD
SUGGESTION. ☺

THIS IS GREAT, GONZO –
YOU POPPED THE FLASH
JUST BEFORE THE SOUP
LANDED ON HIS TIE.

YEAH, WELL,
PHOTOGRAPHY IS AN ART.
YOU'VE GOT TO HAVE THE RIGHT FILM,
THE RIGHT EXPOSURE ... AND YOU'VE
GOT TO **SCREAM** JUST BEFORE
THEY GET THE FOOD IN THEIR MOUTH. ☺

WE'RE GONNA CATCH THOSE THIEVES RED-HANDED.

WHAT COLOUR ARE THEIR HANDS NOW? ☺

IN OUR HOUSE
WE USE PAPER PLATES.

**Every night after
dinner my wife**

ERASES

the dishes. ☺

THIS SHOW IS GOOD FOR WHAT AILS ME.

WHAT AILS YOU?

INSOMNIA. ☺

HEY, RIZZO, RELAX!
DON'T BE SO AFRAID

I'VE GONE WAY BEYOND AFRAID. RIGHT NOW I'M SOMEWHERE BETWEEN **BED-WETTING** AND A **NEAR-DEATH EXPERIENCE.** ☺

"BRAVO! BRAVO! BRAVO!"

TO GO
HOG WILD!

I am paying you to give me help, not cheap jokes. ☺

IF A MAN BORN IN **Poland** IS A **Pole,** IS A MAN BORN IN **Holland** A **Hole?** ☺

YOU KNOW
WHAT YOU ARE,
GONZO?

What?

DISTINCT.

MY DEAR,
YOU ARE SO **BEAUTIFUL.**

HAVE I SEEN YOU
IN THE MOVIES?

I DON'T THINK SO.

I hardly ever go!

DR BOB, CHICKENS DO NOT QUACK.

THEY DO WHEN THEY'RE YOUNG.

THEY DO?

Sure. If you drop
an egg, it'll

QUACK! ☺

GUYS,
I WARNED YOU THIS WOULDN'T BE EASY.
BUT WE HAVE TO
START

SMALL.

THEN
GO HUGE?

THEN GO SLIGHTLY LESS SMALL.
THEN A TOUCH LESS SMALL
UNTIL WE'RE SMALL
TO MEDIUM-SMALL. ☻

HAVE WE GOT ANY NAPPLES?

NAPPLES? YOU MEAN APPLES?

TEN OR ELEVEN MILES AWAY! ☺

YEAH, THAT'S THE
ROAD MANAGER.

HE'S THE MAN WITH
THE CONTACTS?

No, he's the man with the van. ☺

DR. BOB,
DO YOU THINK THE
TELEPHONE NEEDS
ANAESTHETIC?

IF SO,
MAKE IT A
LOCAL.

THAT WRAPS IT UP!

WE'LL SEE YOU NEXT TIME!

[HOLD FOR APPLAUSE . . . .]

WHY?

BECAUSE LONG-DISTANCE COSTS TOO MUCH! ☺

A tap-dancing chicken act?
GONZO, I'VE NEVER HEARD OF ANYTHING AS RIDICULOUS AS A DANCING CHICKEN.

HOW
ABOUT A

**TALKING
FROG?** ☻

YOU THINK THIS SHOW IS **EDUCATIONAL?**

YES, IT'LL DRIVE PEOPLE **TO BOOKS!**

THAT MAN IS ANNOYING ME.

BUT HE ISN'T EVEN LOOKING AT YOU.

That's what's **ANNOYING ME!** ☺

SPEAKING OF CHEAPSKATES, I KNOW A GUY SO CHEAP...
WHEN HE GOES FISHING HE PUTS
A PICTURE OF A **WORM**
ON HIS HOOK,
AND IT CATCHES

A PICTURE OF A FISH! ☺

AS LONG AS I'M HERE, I'D LIKE TO **DONATE** MY BODY TO SCIENCE.

WITH YOUR BODY
IT WOULD BE DONATED TO
SCIENCE
FICTION

HA
HA
HA
HA HAHAHA HA HAHAHAHA

OH, NO, YOU'RE THE ONE WITH THE FUR.
TURN ON THE LIGHT AND SEE FOR YOURSELF.

OOOOH YEAH, I KEEP MIXING US UP. ☻

I've always dreamed of playing the Berlin National Theatre.

ICH BIN EIN BERLINER!

MORE LIKE FRANKFURTER!

Watch it, buster. ☺

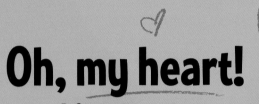

Oh, my heart!

It's going pitter, patter ... pitter, patter.

YEAH, WELL, MAYBE YOU'VE HAD TOO MUCH COFFEE. ☺

I WOULDN'T SAY THE GREAT GONZO IS DUMB,

BUT WHEN HE GRADUATED FROM SCHOOL, HE DIDN'T GET A DIPLOMA — **he got a pension!**

I HEAR YOU COME FROM A BROKEN HOME.

YEAH! I broke it myself!

TWO AMOEBAS WALKED OUT OF A BAR.

ONE AMOEBA SAYS TO THE OTHER,

"Say, is that the sun or the moon?"

I don't know.
I don't live around here,
EITHER! ☺

OH COME ON,

DIDN'T YOU EVEN LIKE

MY LAST JOKE?

SURE WE LIKED IT,

if you promise it's your last one! ☺

I WENT TO THIS BAD SEAFOOD PLACE THE OTHER DAY.

YEAH, IT WAS SO BAD,

THE CATCH OF THE DAY WAS SALMON-ELLA ☺

Kissy-kissy?

UH, MISS PIGGY WHILE I AM FLATTERED AT THIS DISPLAY OF AFFECTION ALLOW ME TO REMIND YOU ONCE AGAIN THAT...

I do not want you.

Oh, good, then can I have her?

(CONT.)

HIIII-
YAH!

THAT IS KNOWN
AS GETTING

**TWO
TURKEYS**

WITH
**ONE
CHOP.**

What music? I mean
REAL BEETLES...
AND SOME TERMITES..... ☺

WE HAVE MUSIC, COMEDY AND 225 DANCING **ELEPHANTS** ...

WHO LEFT THEIR COSTUMES AT HOME BECAUSE UNFORTUNATELY THEY FORGOT TO PACK THEIR **TRUNKS.**

THEY SAY THE CHILDREN OF TODAY ARE THE PARENTS OF TOMORROW.

I thought it
took LONGER
than that ...

WHAT DO YOU GET IF YOU CROSS AN ELEPHANT WITH A RHINO?

WITH A RHINO?

Ella-if I-know! ☺

Here is a
MUPPET
NEWSFLASH!

DATELINE:
The
Muppet Show.

AN EMBARRASSING
SITUATION DEVELOPED TODAY
WHEN THE MUPPET NEWS REPORTER
ACCIDENTALLY WENT ON-CAMERA,

forgetting to put on his trousers ...

Oh, good grief!

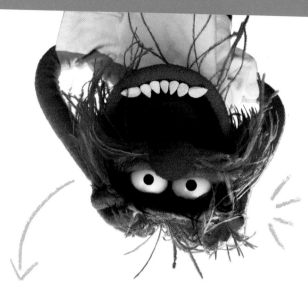

AAAH. You know, I'm falling for you.

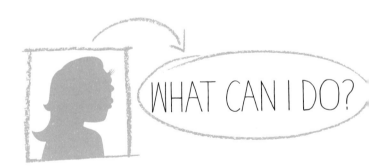

WHAT CAN I DO?

Get out of the **WAY!**
AAAAH! ☺

I CAN, BUT IT JUST HURTS A LOT. ☺

126 Index